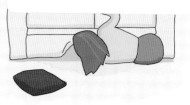

Hang on we've lost something....

You're probably reading this because you've realised something's not going right in your relationship. Maybe you feel the love has gone, or things have got quite stale and somehow your relationship has lost something important. Perhaps you are just going through the motions and it feels like a boring routine? Perhaps there is politeness but a distance, or it feels like all-out war? Or perhaps nasty comments from you both are just slowly driving you further apart? What do you do when for ages you've seen yourself as part of an Us – but more recently there have been problems and it feels like it's just two individuals without the couple?

Whatever has happened to get you to this place, you're possibly now thinking seriously about what to do next.

WHERE ARE YOU?

Be honest...

How would you rate where you are now with your relationship?

☐ I want to get out of it

☐ I'm unhappy

Things are starting to go wrong

☐ We're generally happy

If you're not in a happy place, there are some important decisions to make.

HOW TO USE THIS BOOK

By yourself or preferably with
your partner as relationships
are about both of you.

You may also find the structure
of the book helps you both start
to talk through issues you may
have been putting off.

TIME FOR AN IMPORTANT DECISION

What do you want just now?

Every relationship goes through ups and downs.

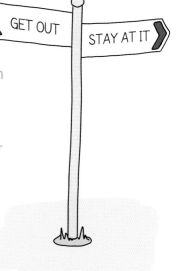

A key question is working out how you respond when things go through a bad patch that seems to run and run.

Most people go into a relationship or marriage wanting it to work. But when things hit the buffers and there's upset all around, there's a hard decision to make.

Either:

- Get out – and leave.
- Stick in there and try to change things around, or find ways of coping with things as they are.

It can sometimes seem that all relationships end in divorce- but that's not true. Difficult times can improve, and you'll know friends who have been in this situation and somehow worked things through.

Get out

Less grief?

Might be happier?

Might find someone better?

Rediscover yourself as an individual?

Maybe you've tried to make changes and you've had enough?

Surely most relationships fail?

Children might be better off?

Time for a fresh start?

SHOULD I GO NOW?

Change things round

More grief?

Might be happier?

Might you find the person you first fell in love with?

Rediscover the US in the You and Me?

Might time and work improve things?

People successfully work through relationship issues every day.

Might children be better off?

You've built up a life together and there's a lot of history.

There's a lot to think about…

BUT BEFORE YOU

Get out
- have you considered ...

Children?

Accommodation – where will you live?

Money?

Have you got somewhere to go?

What about transport?

Mortgage /finance?

Employment?

Practical stuff - e.g. having to drop kids at school.

Emotional consequences – it can be upsetting leaving.

Emotional support – who is there around to help you?

Romance - do you still care for your partner, or is there someone else?

Do you want to leave for today or forever?

DECIDE...

Change things round - have you considered ...

Some people find time changes things.

It's never too late to keep talking.

You may be able to rediscover the passion you've currently lost.

Are you both prepared to put the time and effort in?

Are you prepared to really hear what your partner is saying as well as communicate your own needs?

Are you willing to forgive and leave the past behind?

Are there other things you can do to change things for the better?

How much have you discussed the main issues- really clearly and openly so there is no doubt at all that your partner knows exactly what you are thinking and has had the chance to respond?

It can be easy to think about things that push you apart- how what about things that pull you together?

Have you considered all the options?

A relationship counsellor with expertise and an impartial perspective might allow you to address things you're both finding difficult.

IS THE GRASS REALLY GREENER?

Lust lasts three months

Are you caught up in the idea of leaving or of being with someone else? It can be exciting to fantasise about how someone new might be the perfect answer. But, remember fairy tales tend to end with characters getting together. You don't see what happens next, after the end of the movie. They don't talk about the fact that fairy princesses (and princes) might have smelly feet too!

So:
- Don't decide just based on a fantasy.
- Affairs seem exciting and involve new things, nice places, hotels and sex, but.... living together includes all the boring, mundane days too.
- You may simply not know all the negatives about the exciting new person, so when the honeymoon period wears off, reality can set in and you may realise it's not as good as what you had before.

So, take off the "lust" glasses

REMEMBER WHAT'S IMPORTANT TO YOU

What sort of person do you want to be?

All of us have values about how we want to live our lives. Want to be a trusted husband or wife? Want to be a good role model for your children?

How do you resolve the different tensions involved in making a choice that builds on these things?

Maybe you're someone who prays during difficult times? Maybe you have a personal religious faith that gives comfort? Maybe you're struggling to keep your marriage vows?

How can you bring these different important values into your decision?

ONE PAGE TO GO BEFORE YOU MAKE A FINAL DECISION

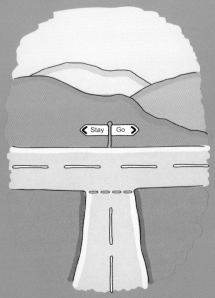

Now, make your choice:

1). Stay and give it a go?

If so, read on…

2). Make a plan to leave?

There are some pages to help you work through the steps needed to do this on page 58.
But before you skip to there, there's nothing to lose from reading on.

Why bother? – Well, because even after you split you're probably going to need to see your ex at least some of the time. If you've built a life together there will be responsibilities which you will need to address together whether this is children, a mortgage, or even bank accounts.

Also, even though your last relationship hasn't worked out, there might be important learning points to consider for the future. Reflecting on what went wrong this time can help you avoid falling into unhelpful patterns next time.

KEEPING THE FRIENDSHIP ALIVE

Don't be just housemates

All successful relationships are built on the foundations of a solid friendship.

In any friendship you'd choose to spend time together.

To:
- Talk.
- Find out what's happening in each other's lives.
- Listen to problems or concerns.
- Compliment one another.
- Laugh together.
- Do fun or crazy stuff together.

It's true of your other friendships- it should be true with your partner.

LEARN HOW TO START OVER AGAIN

You're clearly going through a tough patch. Making an active choice to stay and work at things takes a commitment.

We all start over many times in our lives. Moving house? Leaving your childhood home for the first time? Getting a new job? Leaving a job? Having a child? Starting and ending previous relationships?

It's not so much different this time. Again it's about a choice to move forward together rather than slowly drifting apart.

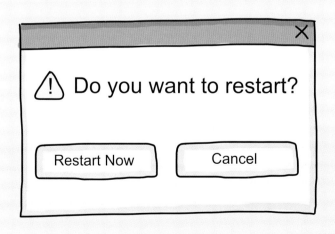

⚠ Do you want to restart?

Restart Now   Cancel

DON'T TAKE THE OTHER PERSON FOR GRANTED

No-one likes to feel like this do they?

- Have you lost the routine of asking what's happened to your partner today?
- How can you show attention and respect?
- Or thanking them for the small things as well as the big things?
- Volunteering to help or take over something which your partner would normally do.
- How can you show that you really appreciate who they are- even if just now it's just certain aspects of them you feel you like.

THERE'S TWO SIDES TO EVERY STORY...

my correct view

your view

Well actually there are three....

Their version.

Your version …

…. and the truth in the middle.

TASK

Pick a time when you've had an argument or been upset by your partner. Really think yourself back into the situation. Who was there? What happened or was said?

Now, turn to the next page and each of you complete what happened from your own viewpoint.

THE EVENTS:

- Where were you? _____

- What were you doing? _____

  _____

- What was said or happened? _____

  _____

- What time of day was it? _____

THE THOUGHTS:

What went through your mind at the time?

- About you? _____

- About the other person? What were they thinking?

  _____

- About the future? _____

- What's the worst that could happen? _____

  _____

THE FEELINGS:

What emotions did you notice?

☐ happy   ☐ sad   ☐ angry

☐ stressed   ☐ anxious   ☐ guilty

☐ embarrassed

What physical sensations were present?

☐ hot   ☐ cold   ☐ sweaty

☐ rapid heart ☐ sick   ☐ tense

☐ pain   ☐ dry mouth   ☐ breathing hard

THE BEHAVIOURS:

☐ withdrawing ☐ shouting   ☐ swearing

☐ criticising ☐ crying   ☐ avoiding

☐ numb   ☐ go get a drink ☐ leave the place

☐ contact a friend)

Other: (add in anything else that's important.)

_____

The next day: did it change how you acted the next day?

_____

YOUR PARTNER'S VIEW

THE EVENTS:

- Where were you? _____

- What were you doing? _____
  _____

- What was said or happened? _____
  _____

- What time of day was it? _____

THE THOUGHTS:

What went through your mind at the time?

- About you? _____

- About the other person? What were they thinking?
  _____

- About the future? _____

- What's the worst that could happen? _____
  _____

THE FEELINGS:

What emotions did you notice?

- [ ] happy
- [ ] sad
- [ ] angry
- [ ] stressed
- [ ] anxious
- [ ] guilty
- [ ] embarrassed

What physical sensations were present?

- [ ] hot
- [ ] cold
- [ ] sweaty
- [ ] rapid heart
- [ ] sick
- [ ] tense
- [ ] pain
- [ ] dry mouth
- [ ] breathing hard

THE BEHAVIOURS:

- [ ] withdrawing
- [ ] shouting
- [ ] swearing
- [ ] criticising
- [ ] crying
- [ ] avoiding
- [ ] numb
- [ ] go get a drink
- [ ] leave the place
- [ ] contact a friend)

Other: (add in anything else that's important.)

_____

The next day: did it change how you acted the next day?

_____

NOW ACT LIKE A DETECTIVE

Yours, theirs
and the truth.

Work out what really happened at the time

Remember we said there were three views to consider.

Yours, theirs and the truth.

You're both the detective. All the clues are in place. Now try and work out together what you both thought- and what really happened?

Do you agree what happened? Interestingly, real detectives know something important. That even trustworthy witnesses remember the same events differently. It's so easy to see what we expect to see, or hear what we expect to hear.

You need to cut through all this and start to really listen. So, stop, think and reflect on how you both responded, rather than jumping to conclusions.

REMEMBER WHY YOU GOT TOGETHER IN THE FIRST PLACE

What was it?

Whether you got married or have lived together, there was something that drew you together in the first place.

Was it:

- Something about their personality? Confident or quieter?
- Making decisions or looking to others for answers?
- Their smile, or sense of humour?
- Their hobbies or interests?
- How you were together?
- Or did they turn you on?
- Their dress sense, hairstyle or how they acted?
- The fact they were a good listener?
- Or any shared interests?
- Or differences?
- Or even how safe and secure they made you feel?

We all inevitably change, the key thing is whether the relationship changes to accommodate that change.

But the thing with change is things that have changed for the bad can sometimes alter again for the better - given time and commitment.

For that to happen, you're going to need something...

YOU NEED AN AGREEMENT

It takes two...

Sometimes it might just be you who is
trying to change things at the moment.

But it's so much easier if you both are
ready for change. If you're both up for
it, read through and sign the agreement
below. If it's just one of you, then you
can sign for you alone just now.

AGREEMENT

I agree I'll:

- Raise issues straight away.
- Not bottle things up.
- Talk to you about problems as they come
  up in our relationship.
- Make time to spend time together.
- Be there as a friend.
- Support you through good times and bad.

Signed _____   Signed _____

But what can
mess things up?

BE OPEN AND HONEST

Say it as it is

How can you or your partner know what the problems are if it's not been said clearly? You may think the problems are obvious, or that you've said it, but have you really?

Clearly and to the point – while not listing every fault you can think of in one sitting.

Being really specific ("When you ignored me on Saturday night it left me feeling…").

Raising issues the person really can change ("I want you to make time just for us").

ASK FOR WHAT YOU NEED

Let's introduce you to three terms

Aggression: where you threaten or bully others to get your own way. You may win in the short term but lose out longer term.

Passivity: where you say yes, when you really mean no. You go along with everything others want, or bend over backwards to please- even when that means you take on far too much yourself.

Assertiveness: where you are able to express your feelings, needs and opinions clearly. You realise you have the right to be listened to, and know that this is important for others too.

If you are assertive, it means you can say yes to the following rules.

How are you doing?

THE 12 RULES OF

I have the right to:

1 **Respect myself** – who I am and what I do. Yes ☐ No ☐

2 **Recognise my own needs as an individual** – separate from what's expected of me as a parent, husband, wife, partner. Yes ☐ No ☐

3 **Make clear 'I' statements about how I feel and what I think** – for example 'I feel uncomfortable with your decision.' Yes ☐ No ☐

4 **Allow myself to make mistakes** – it's normal. Yes ☐ No ☐

5 **Change my mind** – if I choose to. Yes ☐ No ☐

6 **Ask for 'thinking about it' time** – when people ask you to do something, you have the right to say 'I'd like to think it over. I'll let you know by the end of the week.' Yes ☐ No ☐

ASSERTIVENESS

7 **Allow myself to enjoy my successes** – being pleased with what I've done and sharing it with others.

Yes ☐ No ☐

8 **Ask for what I want** – rather than hoping someone will notice what I want.

Yes ☐ No ☐

9 **Recognise that I am not responsible for the behaviour of other adults** or for pleasing other adults all the time.

Yes ☐ No ☐

10 **Respect other people** and their right to be assertive and expect the same in return.

Yes ☐ No ☐

11 **Say 'I don't understand'** so you make sure you work out what is happening.

Yes ☐ No ☐

12 **Deal with others** without depending on them for approval.

Yes ☐ No ☐

Being assertive means having a good plan. You wouldn't want to raise an important or stressful issue just after your partner gets home from work or from the pub. Pick your time and place carefully.

Example:

Sam and Lee have been together for some time. Sam works in a demanding job with long hours and lots of time away. Lee works part-time and also looks after the children. One week Sam is away Tuesday to Friday and gets home exhausted. Lee has also had a tough week- with one of the children ill and off school meaning added pressure.

What doesn't work

Greeting Sam at the door with a list of all the problems.

What would work better

Plan to discuss things the next day and prepare your lines.

PLACE AND PROBLEM

Plan and practice what to say

What's the issue? You're being away all week means I can't keep up with cleaning the house.

What's the impact on you? I'm feeling fed up, and under pressure and am feeling angry you're not able to help.

What do you need? I need some more help around the house. Can we talk through how we can agree something that works.

What's the issue?

What's the impact on you?

What do you need?

WE NEED TO TALK MORE

Starting up conversations again

It's best if you can chat about everything. But to start with you may need to regain the ability to chat about anything.

Use these questions to open up conversations:

What: (e.g. "What did you do today?")

Why: (e.g. "Why do you think our team is doing so badly?")

Where: e.g. "Where do you fancy going on Saturday afternoon?")

Who: (e.g. "Who did you see at the meeting?")

How: (e.g. "How was your day?").

You can follow up any of these questions with other one's that come to mind.

You need to listen too.

HEARING VERSUS LISTENING

Two ears and one mouth?

It's not just about asking questions. Make sure you genuinely listen to the answers too. Give them time to reply and don't interrupt. Notice what they say and how they look and sound. We can listen all day without really hearing a word. To hear is to understand the message somebody is really trying to get across.

But what if you feel you're the only one who is trying to change things? You can't force people to change their personality or to do what you want. Similarly, if someone is unwell with say depression or after a stroke, it's not fair to blame them for the symptoms they now have. But for everything else, you can use the rules of assertion to ask for what you need while bearing in mind some people have never been great conversationalists.

Don't forget you can get the support you need from a variety of people. But be careful who you confide with. Do you trust them to keep things to themselves and do you trust and value their opinion?

So, what gets in the way?

49

THE RELATIONSHIP KILLERS

Things guaranteed to mess things up

- Not spending time together.
- Facing other big external pressures like family illness.
- New children or issues with children as they grow up.
- Getting too involved in new friendships or hobbies that don't include the other person.
- Constantly thinking about being out of the relationship- but in a way that prevents you making the changes you need.
- Drinking too much when you're feeling down or angry.
- Choosing to avoid each other (work, hobbies, children filling the empty gap).
- Arguments about money.
- Not sharing news of the little things each day.
- Picking at faults.
- The silent treatment.

Turn over for adult talk

LET'S TALK ABOUT SEX

Emotional and physical closeness

If you feel close in your relationship, you're likely to also want to feel close sexually. But the opposite holds true too.

If you feel distant from your partner, or stressed out or hurt or angry, you may not even want to be touched by him or her.

If you're feeling like that, it can help to go back to the basics. What about a ban on sex? Instead just start with kisses or a brief hug when dressed and stop there. Over time, if you feel comfortable then you could jointly agree to move on to non-sexual massages, and touch. Think about getting some massage oils or try something new.

You need to both set the pace and you need to agree before you start what your limits are.

KNOW YOUR COMFORT ZONE

Enjoying different things is common

Often when couples drift apart one or other might use porn to provide a sense of sexual satisfaction. Online porn can portray a range of acts which may frighten or push beyond their partners comfortable limits. The same may be true if one partner has experienced and enjoyed different types of sex but this is not shared with their partner. They may want to move the boundaries into areas their partner doesn't want to go.

If you are committed to a relationship the key is to find a comfort zone that you can both enjoy. You need to be open and completely clear about what you enjoy and are happy with. The key is compromise not sacrifice.

Talking about bed..

Never go to bed on an argument, it makes for an uncomfortable night's sleep.

INVOLVE THE EXPERTS

Check out local relationship and marriage counsellors in your community.

Do you need to come with your partner? The answer is usually no - most counsellors will be happy to see just one partner if the other person doesn't feel they wish to attend. It can still be very helpful to talk things through and get a fresh perspective.

Whether you involve an expert or not, if you're planning to stay together, you need to plan to review how things are going every 3 to 6 months to keep you on track and talking.

GOING FORWARD

Summary of key points

1. Think through what you really want. Don't make important decisions based on short term things such as:
   - Lust.
   - Infatuation.
   - Fantasy.
   - Obsession.

2. Look at the whole picture and the implications of any decisions.

3. Base your decision on your values and how you want to be as a person.

4. Most relationships can improve with time, talking and commitment.

5. A key is finding the Us as well as the Me and You.

But if it's time to move on …

MOVE APART — BUT KEEP TALKING

If you have to split ...

... it's good to plan a split amicably. You'll save money (lawyers are expensive) and it will be a lot less upsetting too. Mediation can also help people split up and work through the practical issues like finances.

What if you have children?

If there are children involved, you both need to agree not to drag them into any disagreements. Be aware of trying to win your arguments in front of them. It's not fair on them and they won't thank you for it when they're older. You may be tempted to confide in them and try to persuade them to side with you. That's a dangerous path for all involved.

So, here's some things to try and get right

GETTING THE SUPPORT YOU NEED

It can be a tough time when someone goes through relationship problems or a breakup. You may find you need additional help or supports. You can get more information and support at www.livinglifetothefull.com (www.llttf.com for short).

There are modules on low confidence, anger and irritability, low mood and tension, tackling negative thinking and things you can do to feel happier.

The site is free to sign up and work through linked modules.

It aims to help you live life to the full.

Another Point of View

Contents

Another Point of View

People see things
in different ways.

They make pictures
in their heads
about things that happen.

From these pictures,
they make
their own points
of view.

Points of View

Point of view – number one:
- Skateboarders should have safety helmets, and safety pads, too.

Point of view – number two:
- People have to make their own choices about keeping safe.

What is your point of view? Should all skateboarders have to wear safety gear?

Points of View

Some people said:

- Graffiti looks messy.
It's not street art.
And it takes time
and hard work
to clean it up.

- Graffiti looks *blah*.
And it costs a lot
to clean it off.

Some people said:

- A wall with no graffiti
looks boring.
Graffiti is the art
of a city.

- Graffiti is street art.
For ages and ages,
people have drawn
graffiti on walls.

What is your point of view? Is graffiti street art? Does graffiti look messy?

We aren't upset by gases, and we like it cold.

We don't need air to breathe!

What is your point of view? Could there be life on Saturn?

Getting Other Points of View

Are you good at listening to other points of view?

Do you…

- Listen well when your friends tell you their points of view?

- Give your friends a lot of time to tell you their points of view?

- Help people who are shy to say what they think? Do you ask them: "What do you think?"

- Make sure you let people say what they think without putting them down?

If you said yes to all these, you're a winner.

Ginger Ruth

"I hate my hair!" said Ruth.

"Why do you hate your hair?"
asked Grandma.

"It's ginger,"
said Ruth.

"Nonsense!" said Grandma.
"It's very pretty red hair."

"No one at my school
has red hair," said Ruth.
"The boys call me Ginger."

"Ah, I see!" said Grandma.
"Well, when you grow up,
you can change it, if you want to.
You can change it to black
or brown or blond.
But lots of people like red hair."

"No, they don't!" said Ruth,
and she made a face at herself in the mirror.
But Grandma just laughed.

Ruth combed her red hair.
She pulled out the knots.
The comb had long red hair in it.
Ruth leaned out of the window
and threw the long red hair
as far as she could.

A little bird watched the hair
blow in the wind and fall to the ground.
It flew down and picked up the hair.
Then it flew off to its nest
with the hair.

The next day,
the little bird came again.
Again, Ruth leaned out of the window.
She threw the long red hair
from her comb as far
as she could, and
the little bird flew off to its nest
with the hair.

And so, day after day,
it went on.

The little bird
made its nest
and laid its eggs.
It laid
four little eggs
in the nest,
lined with
Ruth's red hair!

And at school
Ruth was still
the only person
with red hair.
And still the boys
called her Ginger,
and still she hated
her red hair!

In the summer,
four little chicks
hatched.
The baby birds
grew up and
learned to fly.
Soon, they left
the nest.

As it got colder,
the winds came.
One night,
a big branch
blew down.
It came down
with a loud crash
in Ruth's yard.

What made Ruth change her point of view?

The next day
Ruth's grandma went out
to look at the mess.
When she came back,
she had something
small and light in her hands.
"Look, Ruth!" she called.
"I told you red hair is good!"

Ruth's eyes opened wide.
"A nest," she said.
"And it's lined with the hair
that I threw out the window."

Ruth took the nest to school.
When her friends saw it,
their eyes opened wide
and their mouths fell open, too!

They all crowded around Ruth and the nest.
There were people with black hair and
brown hair and blond hair.
But only one person's hair matched
the lining of the nest.

Don't Step on Me!

Written by Etheljoy Smith Illustrated by Richard Hoit

Baxter Beetle combed his antennae.
"I'm off to the library, Beatrice," he said.
"I'm writing a story about humans,
and I have to look up some books.
I want to try and find out why humans
have only two legs."

"Only two legs!" said Beatrice.
"Poor things!"

"Yes," said Baxter.
"And did you know humans
have no wings?"

"No wings!" said Beatrice.
"How horrible!
That means they can't fly."

Baxter Beetle flapped his wings.
"Humans can fly,
but they use a big flying thing
called a...
Oh, Botherbeetle!
Starts with an *a*...
air something...
air... craft.
Aircraft – that's it!"

Beatrice laughed so much
that she fell over on her back
and her six legs waved
in the air.
Baxter helped her up.

"Humans are so funny!" she said.
"Do you think they have antennae
like we have?"

"I don't think so," said Baxter.
"I know they have two eyes and
two ears, and one nose.
I know they have a big mouth
with white things to cut up food.
But I don't think they have antennae.
And I know they have two arms
and flappy things called hands and fingers."

What do
beetles think about
humans?

"Well, please be careful, Baxter,"
said Beatrice.
"I've heard humans
stamp on beetles
and squash them flat.
I wouldn't like it
if you were squashed
flat, Baxter."

As Baxter left his home,
two brothers, Scott and Andrew,
left their home.

Scott and Andrew ran down the street.
They stopped beside a wall.
Baxter Beetle came down the street
at that time, too.

"Great jumping stag beetles!" cried Baxter.
"Two of those humans are right in my way!
And they're the ones that squash you flat!
What should I do?"

The boys got out their marbles.
Then, Andrew saw Baxter's shiny green shell.
"Look, Scott!" he said.
"Look at this big beetle.
Bet you it would make a great big scrunch
if I stamped on it!"

Poor Baxter's six legs shook with fright.
"Don't stamp on it, Andrew!" said Scott.
"It's just a beetle, and it won't bite you.
It just eats plants."

"Well, then," yelled Andrew.
"It's a BAD beetle, and I'm going to stamp on it!"

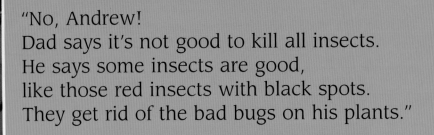

"No, Andrew!
Dad says it's not good to kill all insects.
He says some insects are good,
like those red insects with black spots.
They get rid of the bad bugs on his plants."

"But this insect doesn't have any spots.
It has a shiny green shell,
and I'm going to stamp on it right NOW!"

"Don't stamp on it, Andrew!" said Scott.
"I think that this beetle is a good insect.
What if someone stamped on you?
How would you like to be squashed flat!"

Andrew and Scott have different points of view about beetles. What are they? What is your point of view?

Baxter Beetle looked at Andrew's big feet.
He knew he did not want to be squashed flat.
While the brothers were fighting,
he flapped his wings and flew home.

"I never got to the library, Beatrice," said Baxter.
"But I found out that humans need only two legs.
And you should see all the things they can do
with those two legs. And they have good arms.
Those floppy things at the end can pick up
and hold anything."

"That may be right," said Beatrice. "But, at least, beetles don't need an aircraft to fly!"

23

My Mother's Out of This World!

Written by
Michael Weir
Illustrated by
Fraser Williamson

Hi, everyone!
I'm going to tell you
something AMAZING about my mother.
My mother is not like other mothers.
She LOOKS just like other mothers.
She has the same number of arms
and legs and head parts
as all other mothers.
She's just like your mother, right?
    WRONG!
    My mother
    comes from Mars!

At first, I didn't know
she came from Mars.
Then I found out some strange things.
When we were talking
about what we would do on Saturday,
she said:

"ON THE ONE HAND,
we could go to the beach.
ON THE OTHER HAND,
we could go to Uncle Jack's.
But...
ON THE OTHER HAND,
we could go to the park!"

And I said to myself:
Funny, does my mother
have three hands?

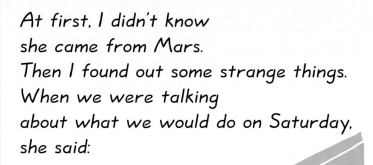

Words have different meanings. What does *to pay an arm and a leg* mean?

When we came home from shopping, my mother said to my father, "I had to pay the butcher AN ARM AND A LEG for the meat today!"

Funny, does my mother have a set of spare arms and legs so that she can swap them for meat or some bones for the dog?

Another strange thing was
when my father said to my mother,
"Would you add up these bills for me, please?
You have A GOOD HEAD FOR NUMBERS."

Funny,
does my mother keep
spare heads?
Does she have a head
with a calculator
for adding numbers?
Does she have a head
for singing songs,
or telling silly jokes?
Does she have a head
for when she is cooking?

Yes, my mother
isn't like other mothers.
She's out of this world.
Only someone from Mars
would be like my mother!
Do you know how I know?
Well, the other day,
I had to call my mother
to the phone.
She was in a room
that I'm never allowed to go in.
And what do you think I saw?
In the room
were rows of arms and legs
and heads and bodies.
And there was my mother.
She was picking out
the best arm
to play tennis with.
So that's how I know!
My mother's a Martian!

Even Grandma knows
that my mother
is out of this world.
When Grandma asked my mother
to give her a hand,
that is just what she did!

What do these
sayings mean?
*A good head
for numbers.
Put your best
foot forward.*

Glossary

antennae – long sticklike parts on the head of insects (or other animals, such as crabs and lobsters) that are used for touching and smelling

bills – papers that tell how much a person owes for things they have bought or for work that has been done

calculator – a tool for working out mathematical problems

graffiti – words or drawings scratched or sprayed on walls and buildings in public places

meanings – what people understand when they think about the words they hear or read

point of view – the way in which people see things in different ways

Saturn – the second largest planet in the solar system

sayings – a group of words written or said often so that they become familiar to people